ROBOT PIONEERS

ROBOTICS IN LAW ENFORCEMENT

CLAUDIA MARTIN

LUCENT PRESS

Published in 2018 by
Lucent Press, an Imprint of Greenhaven Publishing, LLC
353 3rd Avenue
Suite 255
New York, NY 10010

Produced for Lucent Press by Calcium
Editors: Sarah Eason and Harriet McGregor
Designers: Paul Myerscough and Emma DeBanks
Picture researcher: Rachel Blount

Picture credits: Cover: Shutterstock: Digital Storm; Inside: Courtesy AeroVironment, Inc. 18–19, 19b; Carnegie Mellon University 35t; Draganfly Innovations Inc. 16, 17; Lance Cpl. Stephen D. Himes 28; General Robotics Ltd 1, 50–51, 51r; Kimball Hall/ Hydronalix 42–43, 43t; ICOR Technology CALIBER® Robots - www.icortechnology.com 9, 30, 31; Knightscope, Inc. pp. 58–59, 59t; NASA 60–61; NASA/Robert Markowitz 61; © 2017 Northrop Grumman Corporation 21; Shutterstock: Veselin Borishev 56–57, Andrew Burgess 4–5, Ben Carlson 38t, Anthony Correia 32–33, Kobby Dagan 52–53, Deepspace 34–35, Digital Storm 40–41, Dim Dimich 46, Drone Media Studio 48, FeyginFoto 54b, ID1974 33t, i-m-a-g-e 14–15, Glynnis Jones 25, Kasezo 48–49, Sanchai Khudpin 24, Alexander Kolomietz 15b, KPG Payless 41t, Luca Lorenzelli 8, MikeDotta 53b, Jordan Tan 4b, Think4photop 36, Tigristiara 38–39; Smart City Expo 2016 by Sparta Digital 54–55; Wikimedia Commons: ALYaR robotic Ltd. 26, 27, Steve Dock 11, Mark Heeter (USAG Schweinfurt) 57t, Katemcgarry 44–45, Ksp0704 6, MathKnight 7, 47, Necro34 10, NIST 37, Outisnn 12, Simon Q 13, U.S. Air Force photo by Bobbi Zapka 22–23, Photo by U.S. Army Reserve Sgt. 1st Class Lisa M. Litchfield, 319th Mobile Public Affairs Detachment, U.S. Army All-American Bowl JIB 29, U.S. Navy 23t, U.S. Navy photo by Mass Communication Specialist 1st Class Joseph W. Pfaff 44t, Molnár Zsolt 20.

Library of Congress Cataloging-in-Publication Data

Names: Martin, Claudia.
Title: Robotics in law enforcement / Claudia Martin.
Description: New York : Lucent Press, 2018. | Series: Robot pioneers | Includes index.
Identifiers: ISBN 9781534562158 (library bound) | ISBN 9781534562165 (ebook) | ISBN 9781534563018 (paperback)
Subjects: LCSH: Law enforcement--Technology--Juvenile literature. | Robotics--Juvenile literature.
Classification: LCC HV7922.M338 2018 | DDC 629.8′92--dc23

Printed in the United States of America

CPSIA compliance information: Batch #CW18KL: For further information contact Greenhaven Publishing LLC, New York, New York at 1-844-317-7404.

Please visit our website, www.greenhavenpublishing.com. For a free color catalog of all our high-quality books, call toll free 1-844-317-7404 or fax 1-844-317-7405.

CONTENTS

CHAPTER 1

BOMB DISPOSAL

You may not realize it, but many different types of robots are already helping police officers do their work. Some robots help enforce the law by patrolling the streets or tracking down suspects. Others keep people safe by carrying out dangerous rescues or defusing bombs.

Why Use Robots?

A robot is a machine that carries out a series of tasks automatically, without the help of a human. Some robots are completely autonomous. This means the robot gets all its instructions from its own internal computer. A robot's computer is often called its "controller," as it controls all the robot's moving parts. A computer follows a set of step-by-step instructions called a program. A simple program might go a little like this: "Travel to position A," "Turn right," "Travel to position B," "Stop."

Not all robots are completely autonomous. Some are semiautonomous. They carry out tasks programmed into their computer, as well as tasks ordered by a human operator. Bomb disposal robots are usually semiautonomous: a human operator sends them instructions using a remote control, while keeping a safe distance from the bomb.

Thousands of bomb disposal robots are at work across the globe.

Bombs are sometimes made by terrorists. If they go off, they cause explosions that injure people. Sometimes they just damage property and make people afraid.

Robots are used for bomb disposal and other law enforcement tasks because the work is dangerous. Using a machine to make a bomb safe means that a human is not put in harm's way. As well as being mobile and performing a range of programmed tasks with its moving parts, a law enforcement robot is also usually built from very strong materials, including a tough outer covering. This means the robot is less likely to be damaged while carrying out its work.

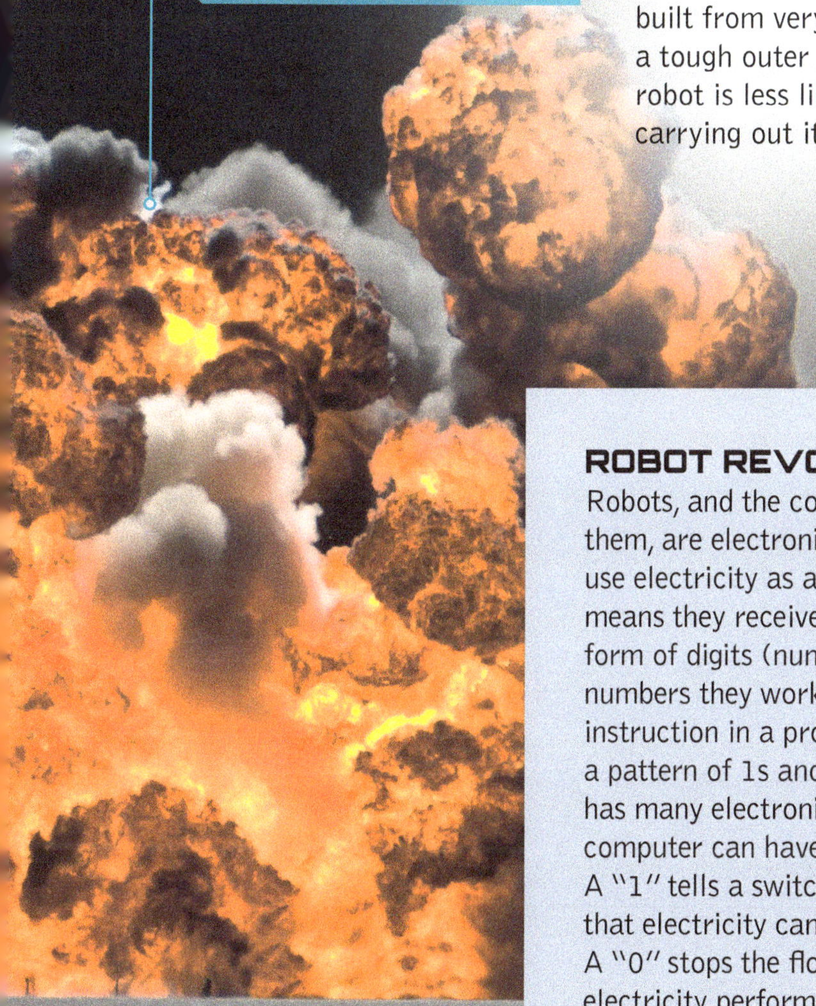

ROBOT REVOLUTION

Robots, and the computers that control them, are electronic digital machines. They use electricity as a source of power. Digital means they receive their instructions in the form of digits (numbers). In fact, the only numbers they work with are 1s and 0s. Any instruction in a program can be turned into a pattern of 1s and 0s. A digital machine has many electronic circuits. A modern computer can have billions of tiny circuits. A "1" tells a switch in a circuit to close so that electricity can flow around the circuit. A "0" stops the flow. Patterns of flowing electricity perform all the computer's tasks, and allow the computer at the heart of a robot to send signals to all the robot's moving parts. The first fully electronic digital robot was invented by George Devol in 1961.

Sensing Danger

Most modern robots have sensors. A sensor gives the robot information, known as data, about the world around it. Without sensors, a robot would bump into things as it moves around. Robot sensors include different types of cameras, as well as sensors that allow a robot to calculate its position or avoid obstacles. Robots are programmed to process the information received from their sensors and to adjust their behavior if necessary.

It is particularly important for a bomb disposal robot to have sensors, as it functions as the eyes of its human operator. The Andros Wolverine bomb disposal robot has several cameras. One camera, which sends full-color video images back to its human operator, is mounted on the robot's moving arm. The camera can tilt and turn, to give the best view. An "ordinary" camera like this uses visible light to capture images.

The Andros F6A is in the same series as the Andros Wolverine. It is smaller, weighing 485 lb (220 kg).

Bomb disposal robots like the Andros Wolverine have saved hundreds, or even thousands, of lives around the world. This robot weighs a full 810 lb (367 kg), about as much as four adult men. It is employed by police bomb squads around the world, including in the New York Police Department. The Andros Wolverine, and its sister robots in the Andros series, are also employed by armies for dealing with explosive devices in war zones. Can you think of any other dangerous tasks that an Andros Wolverine could carry out?

Visible light is just one type of energy. Infrared energy is invisible to humans, but it can be sensed by special cameras. It is given off by anything warm, whether that is a human, animal, or hot mechanical object. The Andros Wolverine's infrared camera converts infrared energy into an electronic signal, which is processed to create a thermal image (an image showing areas of heat and cold) on a video monitor. Its infrared cameras allow the Andros Wolverine to see in the dark.

The Andros Wolverine can also be fitted with other sensors, including an X-ray device. Unlike visible light, X-rays can pass through some solid objects. For example, X-rays travel through skin, flesh, and fabric, but do not travel easily through bones, teeth, or metal. The Andros Wolverine X-ray device allows the robot to see through a fabric, plastic, or cardboard object, like a bag or box, to detect whether or not there is a metal bomb hidden inside.

A bomb disposal robot needs to act as the arms and hands of its human operator. These robots have at least one robotic arm, often called a manipulator. Robotic arms can twist, turn, and lift. This wide range of movement is made possible by a number of joints. The human arm has three joints: shoulder, elbow, and wrist. The shoulder joint allows rotational motion (turning) as well as linear motion (up and down, or left and right). The joints in a robotic arm also allow different types of movement. For example, there are sliding joints, which allow in–out movement, rotating joints, and folding joints. Just like a human arm has a hand, a robotic arm has an end effector. The end effector can be in the form of many different sensors or tools, such as grippers.

Actuators

It is the muscles in your arm that make your joints move. A robot's muscles are called actuators. Actuators make joints and other robotic parts move. Actuators turn electrical energy into movement. A mobile robot usually gets its electrical energy from a battery. One sort of actuator is an electric motor. An electric motor turns electrical energy into movement using the pulling and pushing forces of magnets.

Another type of actuator uses hydraulics. Hydraulic actuators use liquid to make movement. First, the robot's computer opens a valve to allow liquid to flow from a pump to a piston. A piston is a solid bar, which can move inside a tube. The liquid pushes the piston, and the piston extends the arm. Another type of actuator is pneumatic. These work in a similar way to hydraulic actuators but use air instead of liquid.

This bomb disposal robot has two sets of ridged claws. It can carefully hold, lift, and rotate a range of differently sized objects.

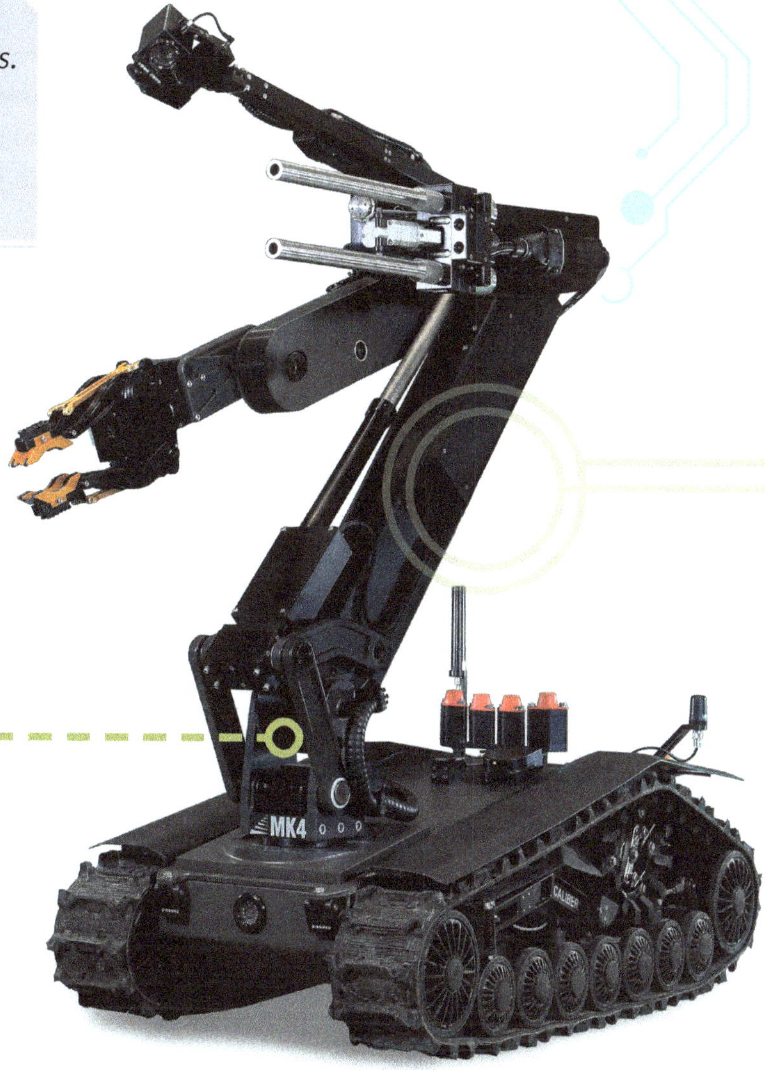

The Caliber Mark 4 bomb disposal robot has a rotating gripper at the end of one of its arms. The gripper can grab and lift securely, thanks to toothed ridges on its surfaces. The grippers are precise enough to open boxes and bags. At the end of another tilting and rotating arm is a camera, which examines a suspected bomb and sends images to the human operator. These images allow the human to decide which is the best method of making the bomb safe. Soon, robots will have the ability to defuse bombs without the help of a human operator. Do you think that is a good idea? Give reasons for your answer.

Mobile robots move in a variety of ways, using turning wheels or running legs, or rolling or slithering across the ground. However, many bomb disposal robots move on tracks. Tracks are bands covered in ridges. They are often found on farm and construction vehicles, as well as military tanks. The tracks' large surface spreads the weight of the vehicle, preventing it from sinking into soft ground. In addition, tracks allow the vehicle to move over uneven ground, up and down curbs, and possibly up steps, without getting stuck.
The ridges give the tracks extra grip. Tracked vehicles are usually slower than wheeled vehicles, but tracks give a bomb disposal robot the stability it needs to perform its careful and highly dangerous work.

With its four tracks, this bomb disposal robot can climb up curbs.

Dragon Runner

The Dragon Runner bomb disposal robot has four wheels, which act as cogs to make its heavily ridged tracks rotate. The robot can reach a speed of 4 mph (6 kph). At just 15 in (38 cm) long and weighing 10 lb (4.5 kg), it is small for a bomb disposal robot. It is built from extremely tough materials, including carbon fibers.

Carbon fiber is a material that is stiff, hard to break, lightweight, and able to withstand high temperatures. It is made from very thin strands of carbon. The Dragon Runner is so tough that it can be thrown down a stairwell or out of a fast-moving vehicle. Not only does the robot remain undamaged, it also does not matter which way it lands. The robot's tracks work either way up, and the robotic arm simply readjusts itself.

The Dragon Runner can travel through deserts or cities.

ROBOT REVOLUTION

Bomb disposal robots make bombs safe in a number of ways. One method is to fire a jet of water at wires on the bomb. Many bombs are powered by electricity from a battery. Knocking away the wires breaks the bomb's electrical circuit and deprives it of electricity. The wires can also be cut with scissor-like end effectors. However, some bombs have a back-up system that makes them explode if their wires are touched. A bomb disposal robot can also carry out a "controlled explosion" by attaching a small explosive to a bomb to separate the bomb's explosives from the detonator (the part that triggers an explosion). Both these methods are dangerous, which is why bomb disposal robots are widely used instead of human bomb defusers.

PackBot

The PackBot 510 is one of the world's most popular bomb disposal robots, with more than 7,000 currently used by police forces, security forces, and armies. Its design makes it highly mobile. The robot's ridged tracks allow it to hold its direction over mud and rocks, and even through shallow water. On level ground, the PackBot reaches 5.8 mph (9.3 kph). The flippers at the front give the PackBot the ability to climb steep slopes and stairs. The action used for stair-climbing is similar to a toddler pulling themselves up step-by-step, using their arms. In narrow or dangerous spaces, the robot can turn on the spot, unlike most vehicles, which have to perform tight turns in several stages. Sweepers and other tools can be attached to the front of the robot to clear obstacles out of the way, or to poke at objects buried in soft ground.

The sturdy PackBot 510 can operate in all weather conditions.

An important part of any bomb disposal robot is its command unit.

When PackBot reaches a suspected bomb, it is equipped with a sensor called Fido, which can "sniff out" explosives. It does this by detecting vapors that would be too faint for a human to smell. This sensor removes the need to risk sniffer dogs, which are trained to smell explosives. The PackBot also sends images to its human operator using its "normal" and thermal imaging cameras.

The PackBot can use its tools, including wire cutters and a hook, to defuse a bomb. In addition, it has a "disruptor," which can fire a number of different projectiles at a bomb, like water, solid shots, and balls that scatter into small pieces on contact. The choice of projectile depends on the bomb design. The disruptor takes aim using a laser, which is a very narrow beam of light that allows pinpoint accuracy.

ROBOT REVOLUTION

Although bomb disposal robots perform many actions automatically, they receive some important instructions via remote control, from a distance of up to 3,000 ft (1,000 m). The remote control has a transmitter that sends the instructions through the air as radio waves. The waves are in a particular pattern, depending on the command. An antenna in the robot picks up the waves. The waves are converted into electronic signals, which can be processed by the robot's computer. The computer then sends the correct electronic signals to its actuators, which create the required motion.

CHAPTER 2

IN THE AIR

Drones, also called unmanned aerial vehicles (UAVs), are used by police forces to get a bird's-eye view of what is happening on the ground. A drone is a robotic aircraft. Instead of having a human pilot, it performs most of its operations automatically.

Around the world, police forces are only just beginning to buy drones, but these robots have already been used to track down people suspected of committing crimes, and people who have escaped from prison. Drones that are used to keep watch are often called surveillance drones. The Federal Bureau of Investigation (FBI) uses a number of drones for surveillance.

A surveillance drone gives a bird's-eye view of city streets.

Cameras

Drones carry video cameras and often they also carry thermal imaging cameras. These detect the warm bodies of humans, particularly at night. Sometimes these drones patrol the borders between countries to keep people from crossing illegally. Thermal images are also useful for locating people who are lost in the wilderness or hurt after a natural disaster. Sometimes, drones even offer practical help in an emergency. For example, in the beach resort of Algarrobo, Chile, drones carry flotation devices that can be dropped for struggling swimmers.

Drones with powerful zoom lenses take images of vehicle license plates, allowing highway patrol officers to catch anyone who is speeding. Where large numbers of people gather for a demonstration, drones can keep watch to make sure no one is hurt in the crush. If someone is trying to disrupt the protest, that person can be pinpointed without obstructing peaceful protestors. Drones can also keep watch over parks, forests, and nature reserves. They make sure no one breaks the law by defacing objects with graffiti, cutting down trees, dumping garbage, or constructing buildings without permission.

This surveillance drone can see through the window into the building.

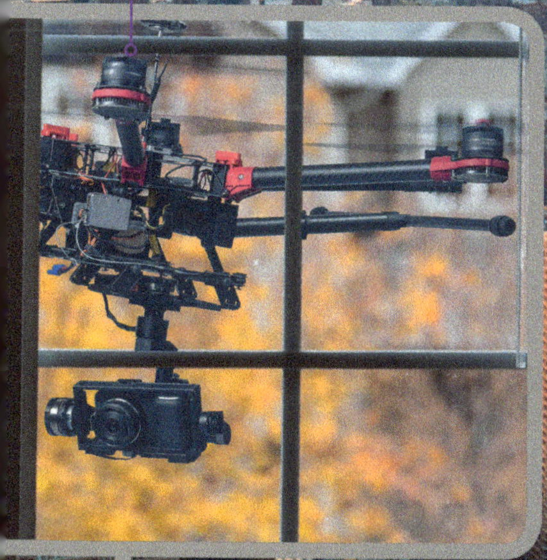

ROBOT REVOLUTION

Like a bomb disposal robot, a drone has two parts: the aircraft and the ground-based control system. Aircraft that are fully operated by remote control are not drones. A true drone is able to perform some functions completely on its own, thanks to its onboard computer and sensors. It can take off and land, avoid obstacles, hover on the spot, and plot its own course. The first robotic drones were developed for the U.S. Air Force in the 1950s and '60s. By 2020, it is predicted there will be 7 million drones flying over the United States.

Helicopters are aircraft powered by turning blades called rotors. The turning of its horizontal rotors makes a helicopter lift into the air and allows it to hover. Helicopters have different numbers and positions of blades. Most large, manned helicopters have one main rotor, plus a smaller tail rotor. Helicopter drones, which are smaller and lighter than manned helicopters, often have four, six, or eight equally sized rotors. These machines are called multicopters. Half the rotors turn clockwise and half turn counterclockwise to prevent the drone spinning out of control. A multicopter changes direction by changing the speed of particular rotors.

Draganflyer X6

The Draganflyer X6 is a multicopter drone with six rotors. With a multicopter design, a small aircraft like the Draganflyer X6 can hover smoothly and is easy to maneuver. Each blade is small and therefore safer for the handler and the public. The multicopter design is not normally used for manned helicopters as it would make them slow to maneuver: The large rotors needed to lift a heavy aircraft would take too long to change their speed. Try pulling paddles of different sizes through water to discover the truth of this: the larger the paddle, the harder it is to maneuver.

A drone's human operator can watch its video as well as monitor data about its height, speed, tilt, and battery power.

In 2014, the Los Angeles Police Department obtained two Draganflyer X6s. A spokesperson from the police department said the drones would only be used in dangerous situations, such as when a criminal or terrorist had taken hostages and lives were at risk. However, many people, including civil liberties groups, were concerned. They said that drones put law-abiding people's privacy at risk. In addition, the police usually need a warrant for surveillance, but drones open up the possibility of watching without permission. Do you think using drones for surveillance should be allowed? Give reasons for your answer.

The Draganflyer X6 is often used for surveillance. Even in high winds, the drone can keep a fixed height and position. It uses its sensors to determine its location and then adjusts its rotors to keep still. The drone's video and thermal imaging cameras are mounted on its underside. This region has been cushioned to be free from vibration caused by the rotors. This keeps the Draganflyer from transmitting shaky images.

Not all drones are helicopters: some are fixed wing aircraft, like a passenger airplane. Fixed wing aircraft stay in the sky because of a force called lift. Gravity pulls an airplane to the ground, but lift keeps it in the air. As a fixed-wing airplane moves forward, wind flows over and under the wings. The air flowing underneath the wings puts more pressure on the wings than the air flowing above them. This pushes the plane upward, working against the force of gravity.

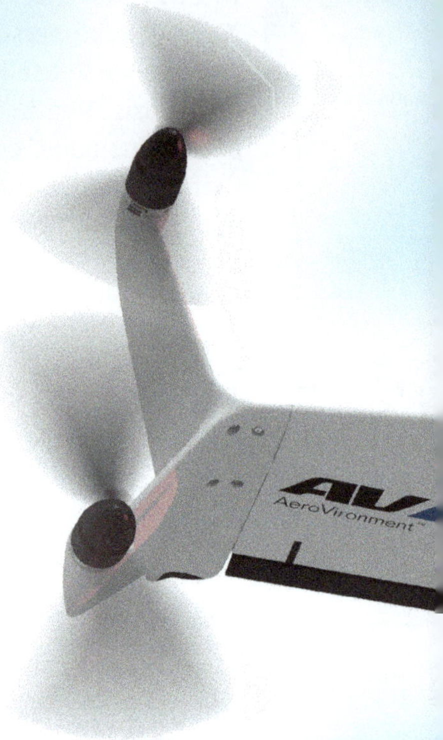

The benefit of a fixed wing drone over a multicopter is that a fixed wing uses up less energy during flight than a multicopter of the same size. This is because a fixed wing gets its lift from its wings and uses its motors only for moving forward. A multicopter has to use its motors for both tasks. All small drones need to have a lightweight battery. As a result, a drone's store of electrical energy is limited. Fixed wing drones are often used for tasks that need longer flight times.

Quantix

One benefit of multicopters is that they take off vertically, while a fixed wing drone needs a much larger takeoff area, as with a passenger airplane. A pioneering drone called Quantix has solved this problem. Its rotors lift it into the sky vertically, with its nose in the air. When it has reached the necessary height, Quantix moves into flight mode by positioning its wings parallel to the ground.

A Quantix's flight plan is programmed before takeoff.

This Quantix drone can fly for 45 minutes. A multicopter drone of the same size and weight could fly for about 25 minutes.

ROBOT REVOLUTION

Drones and other mobile robots use a Global Positioning System (GPS), the same system used by car navigation devices. Around 30 GPS satellites orbit Earth. Every satellite continuously sends out radio signals that give its location and the time. The signals travel to a drone's GPS receiver at the speed of light: 186,000 mps (300,000 kps). Now the GPS receiver knows the location of the satellite, the time the signal left the satellite, the speed the signal traveled, and (from the receiver's own clock) the time the signal arrived. This allows the GPS receiver to calculate the distance to a satellite. A GPS receiver needs at least three satellites to be above the horizon to be able to pinpoint its location.

Drones usually follow a route that is programmed before takeoff. Yet when they are out of sight of their human operator, they must avoid obstacles like birds, power lines, passenger planes, and other drones. There are several different sensors that can help. This technology is often called "sense and avoid."

Drone Sensors

One common system is the Light Detection and Ranging (LIDAR) system, which allows a drone to judge the distance of an object and how fast it is approaching. A LIDAR sensor shines ultraviolet light at an object. Some of the light reflects back off the object. The sensor times how long the light takes to return. By repeating the same operation continuously, a LIDAR sensor provides data on how fast an object is moving.

Interspect is an octocopter, with eight rotors. It can fly at 25 mph (40 kph).

Ultrasonic sensors also judge distance and speed of approach. These sensors use sound waves in a way that is similar to how a LIDAR sensor uses ultraviolet light. Ultrasonic sensors send out sound waves, which bounce off surrounding objects. The time taken for the sound wave(s) to return gives the ultrasonic sensor data to build up a picture of what is around it. Ultrasonic sensors can be used to maintain a steady height by providing data on the distance to the ground. They are particularly useful when landing, so the drone can touch down gently. Navigation cameras also help keep a hovering drone steady. They are programmed to identify and fix on particular details on the ground. When these details change position within the camera's sights, the camera warns the drone that the wind is moving it off course.

The Rotary Bat has a traditional helicopter design. At 12 ft (365 cm) long, the Rotary Bat is larger and heavier than most surveillance drones. This makes it more expensive to power, but offers some benefits. The Rotary Bat can carry loads of up to 44 lb (20 kg) without losing power. With a top speed of 46 mph (74 kph) and a flying time of 180 minutes before its power is exhausted, the Rotary Bat can cover large distances. A human operator can use one control station to monitor several Rotary Bat drones. This is helpful for getting a picture of a wide region, as may be necessary during a hunt for a suspect, or in the aftermath of an earthquake. Can you think of any other uses for the Rotary Bat?

Bigger and Better?

The MQ-8 Fire Scout is one of the world's larger drones. The biggest models are 34 ft 8 in (10.6 m) long. This is the same length as a full-size helicopter, and the Fire Scout costs $18 million to buy. It is not the world's most expensive drone, which may be the fixed wing Global Hawk, which costs at least $131 million and is used for military surveillance. In comparison, a small surveillance drone usually costs a few hundred dollars.

A Global Hawk flies at 357 mph (575 kph).

At present, the Fire Scout works only for the United States Navy. In the future, the drone, and other full-size drones like it, may be employed by a range of police and security forces. As well as having all the necessary "sense and avoid" technology, the drone is equipped with radar (Radio Detection and Ranging). Radar uses radio waves to detect objects. Radio waves sent out from the drone's transmitter reflect off surrounding objects and return to the receiver, giving information about the objects' locations and speeds. Equipped with its up-to-the-minute radar technology, a possible job for the Fire Scout is monitoring shipping traffic for the coast guard, keeping watch for smugglers and pirates.

The Fire Scout has a powerful engine that runs on liquid jet fuel, like an ordinary helicopter. This means it can fly for a full 15 hours. The Fire Scout's larger size means it can carry heavy loads. Some models can carry up to 2,950 lb (1,340 kg). In the future, this would allow the Fire Scout to drop supplies for people stranded in disaster areas. The drone could also pour water onto wildfires. This is a job already done by helicopters with pilots, but using a robotic aircraft might be safer.

The Fire Scout follows a preprogrammed route. Its path can be changed in flight by its human controllers, who work in a central control room. With a machine this heavy and powerful, and traveling with a tank of flammable fuel, the Fire Scout can be operated only by highly trained officers. Do you think the Fire Scout could one day replace helicopters piloted by humans? Do you think a Fire Scout's operators are able to monitor the helicopter as safely as if they were flying it themselves?

CHAPTER 3

GROUND SURVEILLANCE

Mobile robots are used for surveillance at ground level. They are put to work when police officers need to see behind closed doors. This might be the case in a hostage situation, or when suspected criminals are being raided.

Ground surveillance robots provide a picture of the geography of hidden areas and who is inside them. This enables police officers to plan their actions, without putting themselves at risk. The robots send data from their video cameras and microphones to their human operators. Sensors like LIDAR provide measurements of the distances between individuals and rooms.

Some ground-breaking robots can actually "see" through walls. The Cougar 20-H robot sends out very high-energy radio waves that pass through even thick walls. When the waves bounce off objects and return, the robot's computer turns them into images. These signals are so sensitive they even reveal the breathing rate of a suspect by measuring their chest movements.

Most ground surveillance robots are semiautonomous. They perform many of their operations independently, like avoiding obstacles, but a police officer sends them some instructions by remote control. The human operator guides the robot through telepresence technology, using the robot's cameras and microphones to "feel" as if they are present.

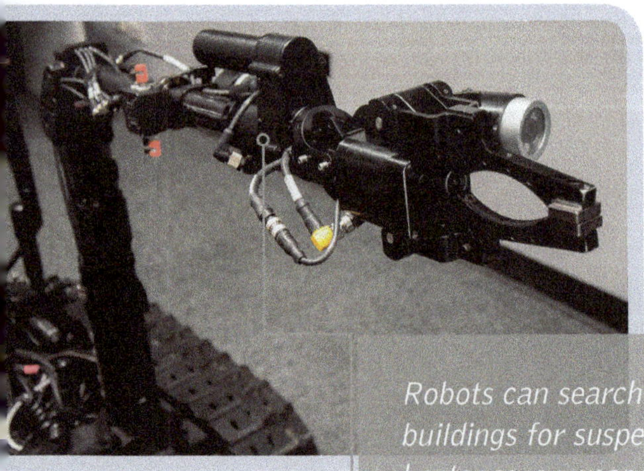

Robots can search buildings for suspects, hostages, or weapons.

The most important tool for a ground surveillance robot is a camera.

A few ground surveillance robots are completely autonomous. They can independently travel into a restricted area and perform tasks like mapping and filming. At present, fully autonomous robots are not programmed to confront suspects on their own. For now, it is believed to be safest to leave the decision-making involved in these tasks to humans.

Artificial Intelligence

A pioneering new generation of surveillance robots will be completely autonomous and will be programmed with artificial intelligence (AI). AI is when computers seem to think for themselves, making decisions and judging the consequences. A surveillance robot with AI will be able to judge the speed at which different suspects are approaching, and make decisions in response, like whether to hide or confront a suspect.

ROBOT REVOLUTION

Computers, and the robots they control, can only do exactly what they are told by their programs. Although artificial intelligence seems to give robots a human-like ability to think independently, it is actually created by programming. AI programs use complicated math to allow a robot to decide between different responses to a problem. AI programs also allow robots to learn from the past and choose the best option in a future scenario.

Stealthy Robots

A surveillance robot must go unnoticed. When designing stealthy robots, engineers often take their inspiration from the natural world. Animal predators, like snow leopards or lions, are usually camouflaged, with bodies that are patterned, colored, and textured to match their environment. They creep silently up on their prey, keeping close to the ground. Most current surveillance robots are small, with dark colors to make them less visible in most environments. An example of a surveillance robot employing these strategies is the Boomerang. It is a small two-wheeled robot that can roll beneath furniture and down stairs. It also has some camouflage, with a matte, textured body that does not catch the light.

For a robot to travel silently, the method of movement is important. The robot's actuators must be highly precise electric motors that make no noise. A robot that rolls along the ground on wheels or tracks will make less noise than a robot that walks on legs. The robot's materials are also important. Wheels made from soft plastics make less noise than spiked metal wheels.

With its subtle camouflage, Boomerang can stay hidden in urban or wild environments.

The next generation of surveillance robots will take stealth to a new level. An experimental robot made by pioneering researchers at Harvard University opens up interesting possibilities. The robot has a soft rubbery body that can squeeze silently through small gaps. It is also covered in tiny tubes. Dyes are pumped in to change the robot's coloration in an instant. Patterns can be created. In addition to changing color, hot and cold liquids can be pumped in to match the air temperature. This enables the robot to be invisible to thermal imaging cameras.

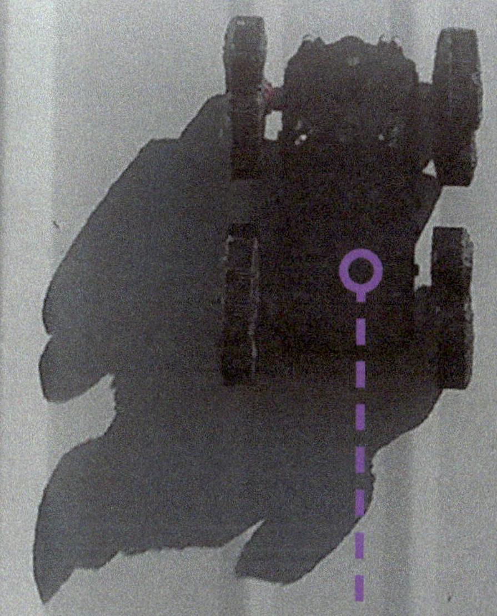

The Magma surveillance robot has magnetic wheels. This means it can climb up metal structures, like lampposts and pipes. The small, lightweight robot is also waterproof and can be steered over metal surfaces under water. It is armed with full-color video cameras and bright lights to illuminate hidden places. Do you have any concerns about using stealthy robots like Magma?

Throwable Robots

These robots can be hurled through open windows, over fences, and onto rooftops. A throwable robot's frame and sensors must be strong enough to survive the impact. Today's throwable robots are also mobile. They often have two wheels, with a symmetrical body running between them. The robots' center of balance is exactly in the middle. Whichever way up these robots land, they can immediately roll off to the right spot for surveillance.

Designed for use by armies and security forces, Stingray is lightweight and speedy.

The Throwbot XT is one of the world's most advanced throwable surveillance robots. It is 7.6 in (19.3 cm) wide from wheel to wheel. It weighs just 1.2 lb (540 g), which makes it easy to throw long distances—up to 120 ft (36 m). The robot is strong enough, and its rubbery surfaces are absorbent enough, for the robot to withstand vertical drops of 30 ft (9 m). If the robot accidentally falls into water, it can be submerged for up to 5 minutes without the water affecting its ability to function.

Once the Throwbot XT has landed, it is directed by a human operator to roll silently through any structure, sending back video to the operator's hand-held command unit. In darkness or low light conditions, the video camera automatically switches to using infrared, so the operator can see in the dark. The robot also has sensitive microphones for listening in on conversations. Up to three Throwbot XTs can be monitored by the same operator, as one command unit can send and receive instructions at three slightly different frequencies (using three different patterns of radio waves). The Throwbot's lightweight battery allows it to move and run its sensors for up to one hour.

ROBOT REVOLUTION

After the Boston Marathon bombings in 2013, the terrorists who carried out the attack went on the run. The public used social media to help the police track them down, posting videos, photos, and reports of sightings. Social media is websites where users can interact with each other, like Facebook, Twitter, and Instagram. Inspired by events like this, today's pioneering surveillance robots can monitor social media. They look for keywords, particular faces in videos, and hashtags on Twitter. They compare this data with real-time events monitored through video and other sensors. This technology helps track down suspects and could even prevent crimes before they happen.

This is the Throwbot XT, a pioneering throwable robot.

Opening Doors

Some of today's surveillance robots do more than just look and listen. They can also open doors and pick up objects. One of these pioneering robots is the Mini Caliber. At 24 in (61 cm) long and 16 in (41 cm) wide, it is larger than most surveillance robots. However, with a weight of 64 lb (29 kg), it is still light enough for an adult to carry it to the site of operations. The Mini Caliber needs its extra size to give it reach and strength. Its extendable arm can reach 66 in (168 cm) high and 52 in (132 cm) across.

A Mini Caliber is carried to a raid on a suspect's home.

The Mini Caliber arm's end effector is a claw that rotates 360 degrees (a full circle). This allows it to turn doorknobs with as much control as a human hand. The arm is also fitted with a video camera, which switches automatically to infrared in darkness. A Mini Caliber has a range of extra tools that can be fitted to the arm in place of the claw: blades on claw tips for opening boxes, tire slashers, clothes cutters for finding concealed weapons, a hook for pulling objects, and a disruptor for firing projectiles at bombs. Another camera, on a mast at the back of the robot's body, films the action of the arm, so the human operator can monitor how well the chosen tool is working.

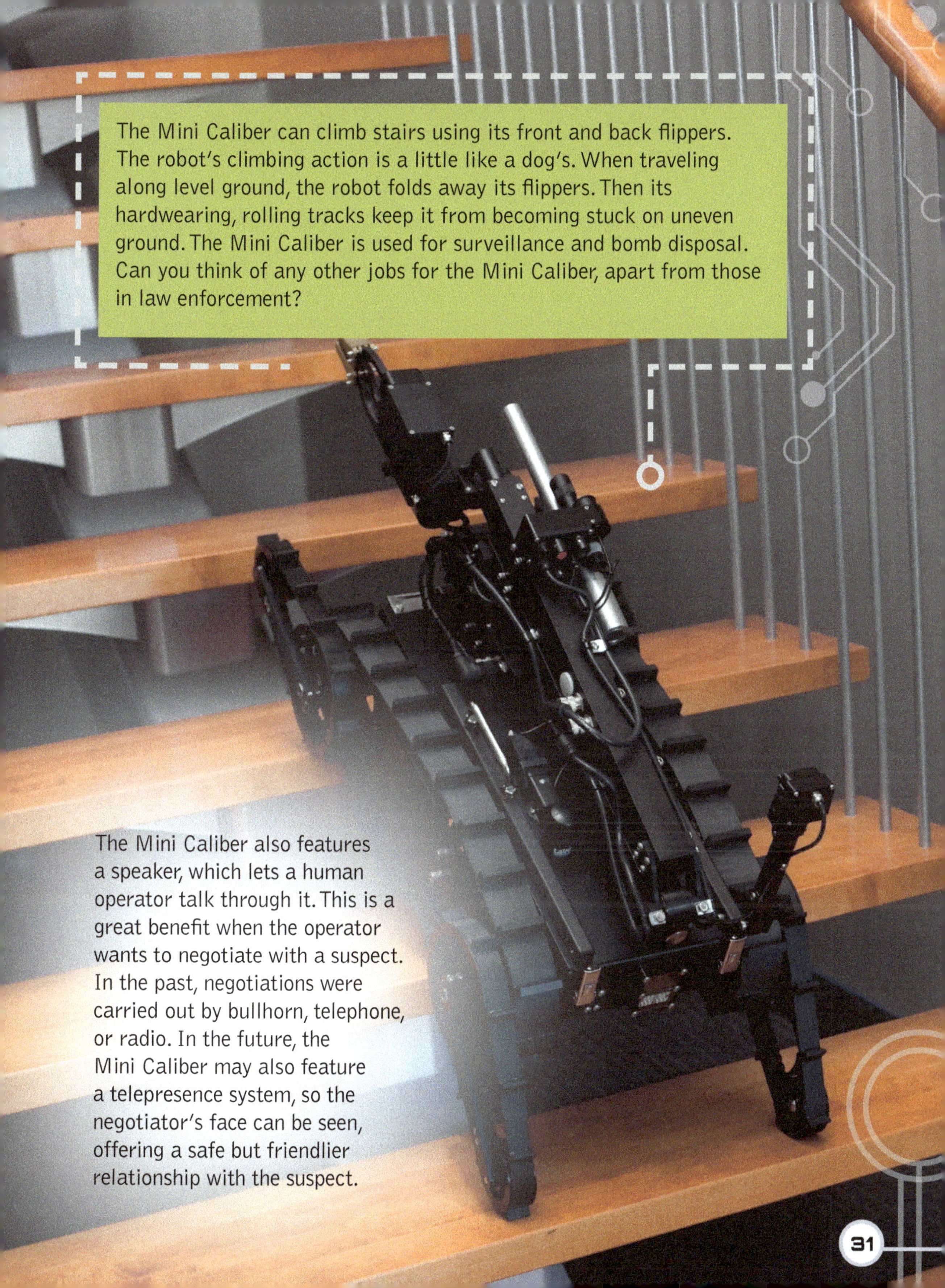

The Mini Caliber can climb stairs using its front and back flippers. The robot's climbing action is a little like a dog's. When traveling along level ground, the robot folds away its flippers. Then its hardwearing, rolling tracks keep it from becoming stuck on uneven ground. The Mini Caliber is used for surveillance and bomb disposal. Can you think of any other jobs for the Mini Caliber, apart from those in law enforcement?

The Mini Caliber also features a speaker, which lets a human operator talk through it. This is a great benefit when the operator wants to negotiate with a suspect. In the past, negotiations were carried out by bullhorn, telephone, or radio. In the future, the Mini Caliber may also feature a telepresence system, so the negotiator's face can be seen, offering a safe but friendlier relationship with the suspect.

CHAPTER 4

SEARCH AND RESCUE

Search and rescue robots help find survivors after natural or human-made disasters. They can enter environments that are unsafe for humans, using their sensors to find people who are trapped or injured.

Natural and human-made disasters both result in the need for search and rescue personnel and robots. These are employed by police forces, as well as by fire services and coast guards. Natural disasters include earthquakes, floods, and hurricanes. Human-made disasters include bombs and car crashes. In addition to these disasters, search and rescue missions are used to find missing people. Climbers and hikers sometimes get lost or hurt in the wilderness. Children and the elderly occasionally get lost in cities. Boats capsize or sink while far out at sea.

Robot Rescue

Although the use of search and rescue robots is fairly new, several types of robots are already being used. Drones can act as an eye in the sky for locating missing persons and identifying areas worst hit by a natural disaster. Full-size helicopter drones can even drop supplies or lift people to safety. Ground-based robots can create three-dimensional (3D) maps of disaster areas and assess the safety of damaged structures. They can crawl into piles of rubble and use their sensors to find survivors. Extra-strong mobile robots can even carry survivors from the scene.

Search and rescue robots may work individually, or they can work as a group, sending and receiving messages with each other and a central computer control system. Although current search and rescue robots are semiautonomous, the next generation of robots will be programmed to carry out rescues alone.

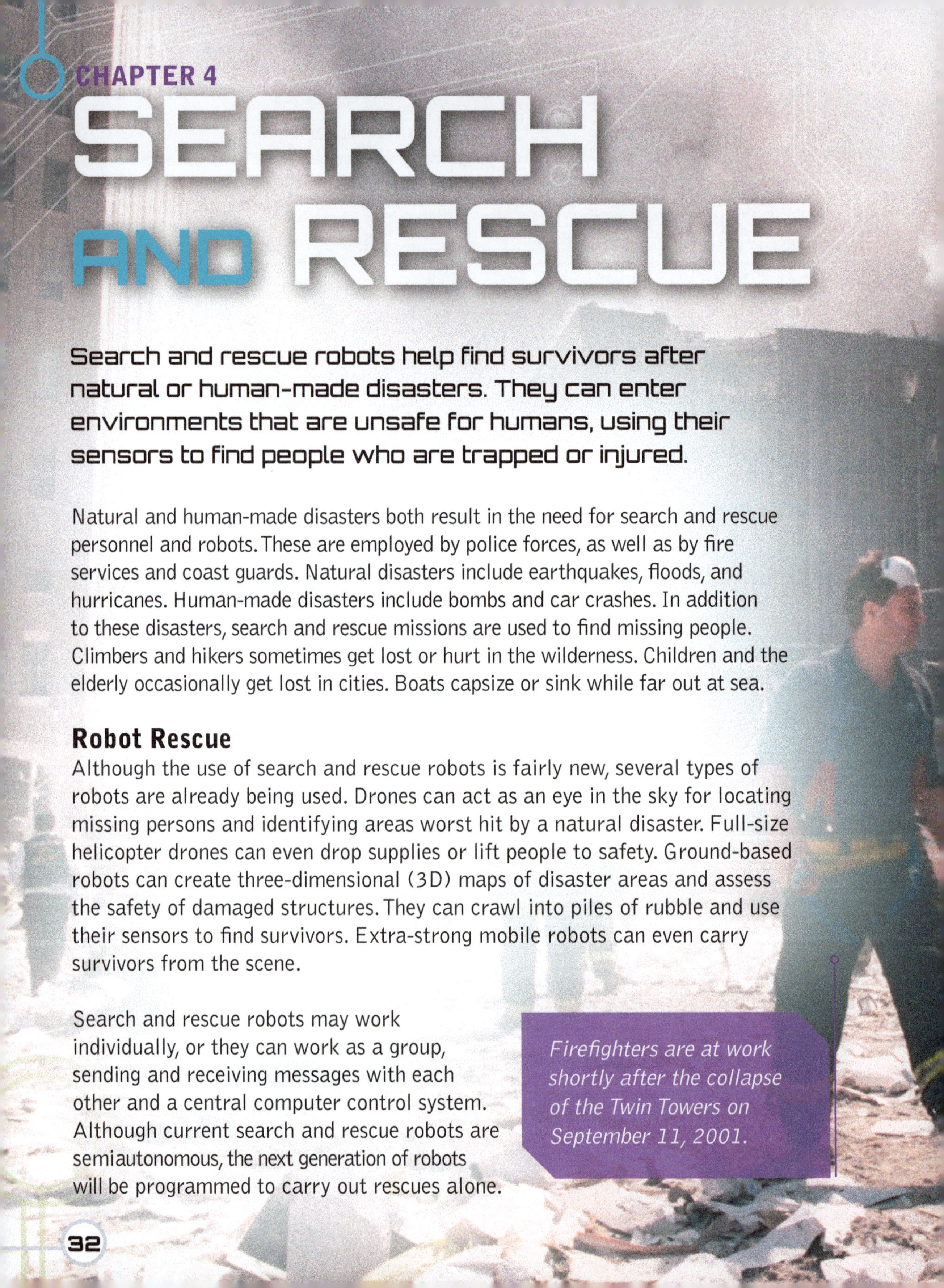

Firefighters are at work shortly after the collapse of the Twin Towers on September 11, 2001.

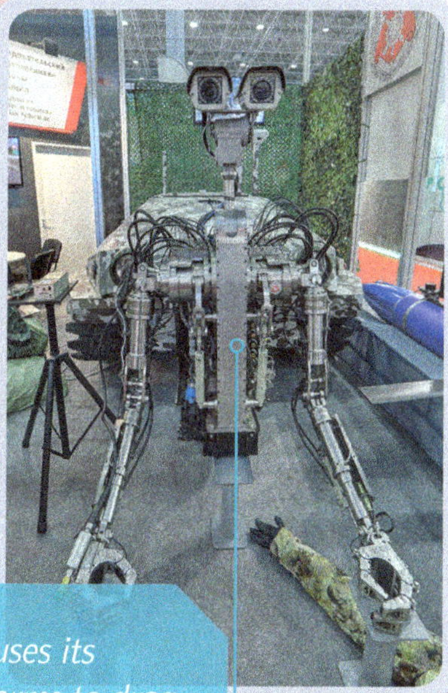

This robot uses its hands and arms to drag injured people to safety.

ROBOT REVOLUTION

On September 11, 2001, terrorists from the group Al-Qaeda flew two passenger planes into the Twin Towers of the World Trade Center in New York. Within 1 hour 42 minutes, both 110-story towers had collapsed, with hundreds of people trapped inside.

The World Trade Center disaster was the first time robots were used to help with search and rescue. Several robotics experts were on the site within hours, including a team from the Center for Robot-Assisted Search and Rescue at Texas A&M University. This terrible event gave the experts a harrowing opportunity to see what their robots could do, but also how much work needed to be done to create robots that could navigate dangerous spaces and save lives without getting stuck, breaking, or losing communication. Sadly, the robots were not able to save anyone. Since then, the technology has grown much stronger.

Following a disaster in which buildings have collapsed, it is vitally important to find anyone trapped inside. The problem is that shifting the rubble even a little can result in further collapses. Rescue workers often pick away rubble by hand, while calling inside and listening carefully for any response. Search and rescue dogs are also employed in situations involving collapses, including snow avalanches and mudslides. Search and rescue dogs of this type are called air-scenting dogs. All dogs have a powerful sense of smell, but rescue dogs are highly trained to pick up human scent. When the dog finds the scent, it barks to alert its human handler. But imagine if a robot could find people trapped in rubble, without any risk to humans and animals.

Snakebots

Snake-shaped robots could be a solution to the problem. Without wheels, legs, or tracks, a snake-shaped robot is less likely to get stuck in rubble. It can also wriggle through tiny gaps. Several snake robots are currently in development. One, designed by researchers at the Georgia Institute of Technology, Atlanta, was inspired by the sidewinder snake, which can wriggle up sand dunes without slipping back down. The engineers watched closely the way the snake increases the area of its body that is in contact with the ground as it goes uphill.

To find trapped survivors, a snake robot would need to be armed with sensors. Similarly to a dog sniffing human bodies, a special sensor can "sniff" the carbon dioxide gas that humans breathe out. There are several different ways that sensors can detect carbon dioxide. One makes use of infrared light. Different gases absorb different amounts of infrared light. This fact allows a sensor to pick out a particular gas.

Rescue workers and sniffer dogs search the rubble after an earthquake.

This snake robot was designed by the Robotics Institute at Carnegie Mellon University, Pittsburgh. Each of the robot's many joints allows it to bend in several directions. The robot can roll sideways, climb up a pipe by curling around it, wriggle forward, and hold one end upright like a head. It is strong enough to shift small pieces of rubble, and can inch through narrow spaces. On top of all this, the robot can swim, using a similar motion to a sea snake. Consider the movement of other animals. Which other means of locomotion might be useful for law enforcement robots? Give reasons for your answers.

Sensing Life

Rescue robots are armed with many sensors. Sensors designed to find survivors include infrared cameras. These provide thermal images that reveal a human's warm body. Another type of sensor that uses infrared energy is called pyroelectric. A pyroelectric sensor makes an electric charge when it is exposed to heat in the form of infrared energy. These sensors can be designed particularly to respond to human bodies, which give off a certain amount of infrared energy. The electric charge can set off an alarm back at the human operator's control station.

Soldiers look for survivors in a collapsed building in Nepal, in 2015.

When it finds a human, a rescue robot needs to show its operator exactly where the survivor is located. This can be done through the robot's GPS, which pinpoints its position on Earth. A GPS can act as a tracker, with the robot's position constantly shown on a computer control screen in the form of a flashing blip. A whole team of robots can be easily tracked in this way.

In addition, a rescue robot needs sensors that provide a picture of the structures and spaces inside a collapsed building or rockfall. This allows human rescuers to safely find their way in later. Devices used to judge the size and shape of structures include LIDAR. Stereovision cameras also enable a robot to create a 3D map. Stereovision cameras work a little like human eyes. Our eyes are located a small distance apart, so our brains receive two slightly different images of any object. The differences between the two images are processed in the brain, giving us an idea of an object's 3D structure. Stereovision cameras also record images from two slightly different locations. Like the human brain, a stereovision program compares the two images, building up a picture of depth and distance.

This rescue robot crawls into tight spaces using its flippers. Rubble-crawling robots need to have sensors that help them keep their balance and know which way is up. One common sensor is a gyroscope. This is a disk that is free to tilt and turn within its container. The gyroscope alerts the robot's computer to changes in angle. The computer responds by sending signals to the robot's actuators. The actuators keep the robot upright by tipping the robot in the opposite direction. Do you think robots will take over completely from humans and dogs in the field of disaster rescue?

After a chemical spill, it is better to send in robots than to risk human workers.

Not all robots that work in search and rescue are small. Some are large, powerful machines. These robots are often called "heavy rescue" robots, which means they are designed to lift, cut, and carry after a disaster or car accident. Tools on these robots' end effectors include cutters, spreaders, and large hooks. These are called breaching tools, because they break into structures. Heavy rescue robots are covered with a tough shell, similar to the armor found on military tanks. This keeps them from being damaged in hazardous environments like in a factory after a chemical spill.

Powerhawk

One pioneering heavy rescue system is the Powerhawk, which consists of a robotic arm and end effectors. The robotic arm is fitted onto robots like the Andros Wolverine. This has the benefit of combining a powerful manipulator with a highly mobile base.

This heavy rescue robot can force rubble out of the way like a snowplow. It is also armed with powerful spreaders.

ROBOT REVOLUTION

On March 11, 2011, a massive earthquake and tsunami struck Japan. They damaged the Fukushima nuclear power plant so severely that radioactive material leaked out. A nuclear power plant uses radioactive material to create electricity. If radioactivity leaks out, it severely damages human bodies. The area around Fukushima was evacuated. To assess the damage, robots were sent into the plant. The 710 Warrior sucked up radioactive dust for testing, using a vacuum cleaner end effector. The highly mobile Quince 2 supplied video of damaged structures. PackBot 510s lifted and removed heavy radioactive materials.

One area where robots are becoming more and more common is firefighting. Even though human firefighters are equipped with fireproof suits and breathing apparatus, they risk their lives every time they enter a burning building or a wildfire. Humans can become disoriented by smoke or trapped by falling ceilings. Robots may offer the solution.

At present, most firefighting robots are remotely operated by a human firefighter. They are used mostly in situations that would be extremely dangerous for a human, like when a tanker of fuel might be about to explode. There are already a few hundred water-spraying robots in use around the world. One of these is the Fire Ox, which carries its own tank of water and has sprayers that send jets of water many feet. Like all driverless vehicles, it has "sense and avoid" technology, such as LIDAR, to help it avoid obstacles.

Humanoid Firefighters

Another firefighting robot is a humanoid. Humanoid robots are shaped like a human, with a head, arms, body, and legs. This robot is the Shipboard Autonomous Firefighting Robot (SAFFiR, pronounced "safer"). It is designed for use on board ships, but has not yet been put to work. Since SAFFiR will be working in tight spaces designed for the use of humans, it makes sense to shape it like a human. Fires on board ships are a particular danger, as evacuation is difficult. SAFFiR will patrol ships, detecting fires using heat and smoke sensors. It will use fire hoses to put out fires, working side-by-side with the ship's human crew. SAFFiR's complex programming will enable it to speak and gesture to humans.

Before long, robots may make it unnecessary for firefighters to risk their lives.

This Japanese robotic fire rescue truck can drag an unconscious person onto its platform. First, the platform is angled until it touches the ground. Then the robot extends its two arms, placing the "hands" in the person's armpits. It hauls them up onto the platform. Then the platform slowly retracts inside the robot. There is room inside for the person to lie comfortably. The person can be carried out of the building, safe from fire and smoke. The human operator uses the robot's infrared and ordinary video cameras to monitor and direct it. Can you think of any other dangerous situations where such a robot could be used? Give reasons for your answers.

A Lifesaver

A robot called EMILY (Emergency Integrated Life-Saving Lanyard) is a lifeguard. The robot is used when someone falls into the ocean, is caught in a flood, or gets into trouble when swimming off a beach. EMILY motors to the rescue from the shoreline, or is thrown from a boat or aircraft. When the robot reaches a struggling swimmer, the person must cling onto EMILY's ropes to be carried to safety. Human lifeguards can swim to the rescue at up to 4.5 mph (7.2 kph), and are slowed by waves. EMILY speeds over the waves at up to 22 mph (35 kph). It can travel for 80 miles (130 km) without needing to recharge its battery. EMILY does not have a turning propeller or rudder that could hurt a swimmer.

The current version of EMILY relies on a human operator to guide it to a swimmer. The robot's developers are working on an upgraded version that will find struggling swimmers by using its microphones to listen for the flailing underwater movements that signal someone is in trouble. The microphones will be sensitive enough to distinguish between happily splashing children and those who are genuinely in need. Sonar will be used to avoid collisions with other swimmers and sea creatures. Sonar is a system that detects objects under water by sending out sound pulses and measuring how long they take to bounce off objects and return. The upgraded EMILY will also monitor water conditions, such as powerful currents that can drag swimmers out to sea.

In addition, the new version of EMILY will patrol beaches, using its speakers to warn swimmers of changing conditions so they can leave the water. When performing a rescue, EMILY's speakers will tell a swimmer to keep calm and instruct them how to use the device.

EMILY is brightly colored and marked by a tall flag, to make it easier to spot in stormy waves.

EMILY is used by the Greek coast guard to carry out rescues in the Mediterranean Sea. After civil war broke out in Syria in 2011, many desperate Syrians fled in boats, trying to reach the safety of Europe across the sea. The boats were overcrowded and unsafe, and thousands of people drowned. In 2016, EMILY was put to work saving the lives of these refugees. One drawback of EMILY is that a swimmer who is unconscious cannot grab onto the robot's ropes. In this chapter, have you read about any technology that could solve this problem? Explain your answer.

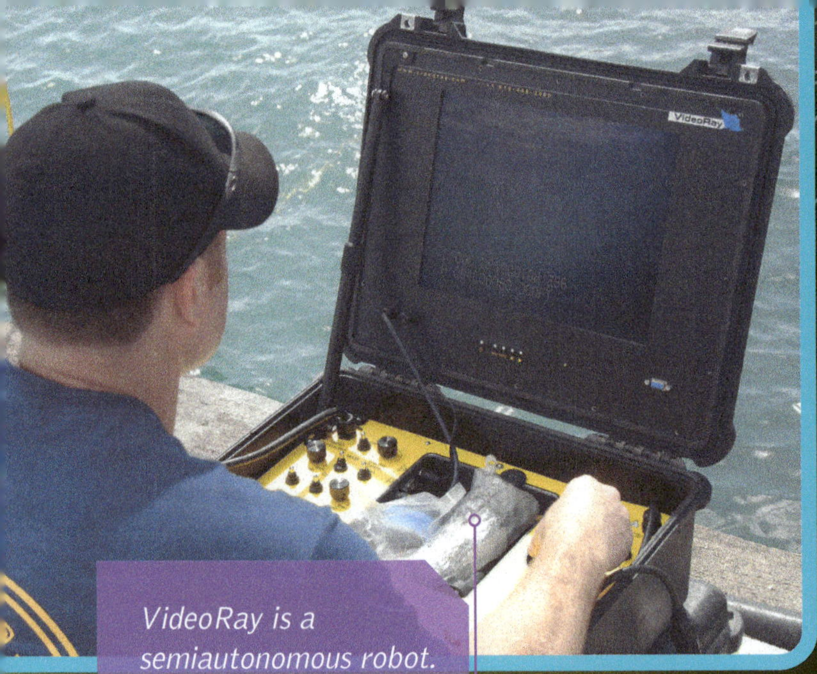

VideoRay is a semiautonomous robot.

Some robots are at work below the waves instead of above them. One underwater robot, called VideoRay, carries out searches. VideoRay's job is to examine underwater structures like harbors and piers. It can inspect damage after earthquakes, as well as monitor disasters like oil spills. Oil spills happen when a large ship carrying oil, called an oil tanker, is cracked and starts to leak fuel. This can kill thousands of sea creatures and birds, as well as damaging ecosystems such as coral reefs. Just as with disasters on land, a damaged environment is dangerous for human divers. The VideoRay's cameras can safely give human disaster response teams the information they need to put a plan in place.

VideoRay is also used for salvage operations. This is when sunken ships or their contents are lifted from the seabed. Sometimes, wrecks are left on the seabed, even for hundreds of years. VideoRay is often used by teams of underwater archaeologists, people who study the past by examining shipwrecks and other sunken remains. VideoRay can swim through portholes and down hatchways, where human divers cannot safely venture.

To avoid collisions and assess the size of underwater spaces, VideoRay uses sonar. A depth sensor, gyroscope, and compass tell the robot and its human operator exactly where it is and which way up it is facing. The robot receives some commands from its human operator, which travel from the operator's control unit down VideoRay's lengthy wire. VideoRay also performs many functions automatically, like holding one position, without being pushed aside by water currents. If the human operator spots particular damage that needs investigating, they can click on that spot on the computer screen. VideoRay makes straight for the location, automatically finding a safe route.

ROBOT REVOLUTION

VideoRay robots were used for the largest and most expensive underwater salvage job that has ever taken place. The cruise ship *Costa Concordia* capsized in 2012, with 4,252 people on board. As they tried to evacuate the ship, 32 people died. The huge wreck could not be left where it was as it was a hazard to shipping and a source of pollution. Seven VideoRays were the eyes of the salvage team, the first time that underwater robots had been used for such an immense task. They recorded more than 45,000 hours of video of the wreck. With the help of those images, the ship was taken apart and recycled by the end of 2016.

VideoRay examines a shipwreck.

CHAPTER 5

USING WEAPONS

At present, most law enforcement robots do not carry weapons. In fact, they are used in dangerous situations to avoid a human officer having to protect themselves with a gun. However, a few law enforcement robots can fire bullets or drop missiles from the sky.

Science fiction is filled with police robots that independently fire their guns. However, in real life, very few weapon-carrying law enforcement robots have been designed. Almost none of them have been put to work around the world. In some countries, weapon-firing robots designed for warfare are occasionally used by police. At present, the decision to fire the weapon is always made by the robot's human operator, not by the robot itself.

Dangerous Robots?

In the United States, the first—and, so far, only—killing of a human by a police robot took place in Dallas, Texas, in 2016. When the robot was deployed, the man had already shot dead two police officers, while three more later died in the hospital. The Dallas police chief was desperate to end the gun battle without losing more officers. He sent a remotely controlled Andros Mark 5A1 bomb disposal robot toward the man, carrying explosives. The man was killed instantly. Many people were horrified by the use of a robot to take a life, while also being horrified by the man's actions.

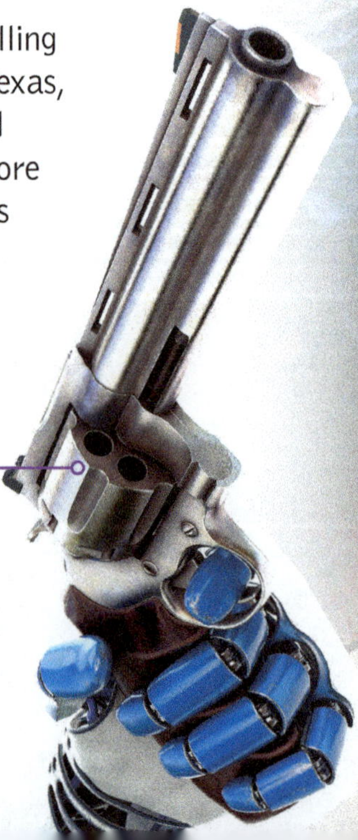

In the future, will weapon-carrying robots patrol our streets?

Several moral questions are raised by giving robots the ability to use weapons. When a weapon-firing robot is remotely operated, does the human operator take the decision to pull the trigger as seriously as if they were face to face with another human being? If robots were allowed to fire their weapons automatically, without receiving the command from a human, could a machine's decision-making ever be as careful and sensitive as a human's? Could a robot make a mistake that a human would not? On the other hand, fearing for their own life, could a human make a mistake that a robot would not?

ROBOT REVOLUTION

Robots used in warfare by armies and air forces were the first to be armed with weapons. Today, the most common armed robots are drones, which fire missiles at enemy targets. At present, the decision to fire the weapon is always made by a human operator. One of the first robots that can automatically fire its own weapons, without human input, was put into service in 2010. It is a Samsung SGR-A1 sentry robot, which guards the border between North and South Korea, two countries with a history of conflict. However, the robot has never yet been allowed to fire autonomously.

Drones are quite widely used by police forces to keep a watch over large demonstrations and riots. Riots are violent public disturbances where property is damaged and people may be hurt. Nearly all these drones are programmed only to send images to their human operators so that police chiefs can make decisions about how best to keep the peace. However, a small number of drones have been designed to put a stop to riots in a different way.

Riot Control

The Vinveli riot control drone can drop nonlethal grenades onto a crowd. The drone is not intended to hurt people but to prevent people being hurt if a riot continues to get out of hand. Grenades are small exploding devices. The riot control drone can drop grenades filled with tear gas, which irritates the eyes. Tear gas has been used to control riots for many years. The drone can also drop clouds of powdered dye, which marks the rioters so they can be arrested later. Flare grenades make a surprising bright light. Faint shock grenades release an electric charge but do not cause casualties.

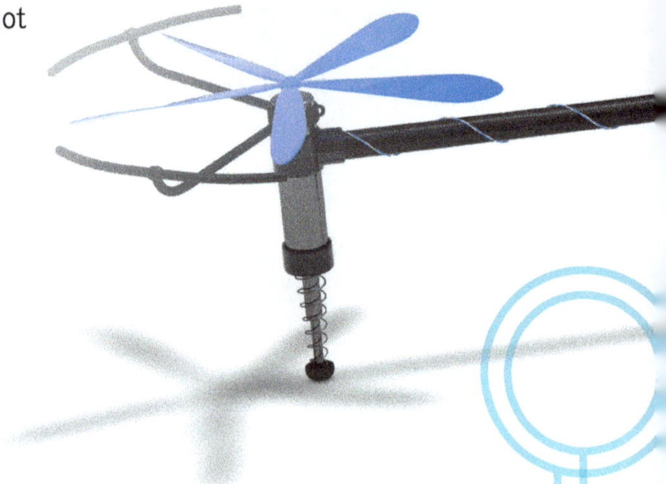

A drone took this photo of a clash between refugees and border police.

Some people are worried by the invention of riot control drones that are equipped with weapons, even if those weapons are not intended to kill. The right to protest peacefully against government decisions and laws is an important right in any democracy. This is one way that governments can be held to account by their citizens. One government may respect its citizens' right to protest, while another may crack down violently on any opposition. Governments do not need armed drones to stop protestors if they have armed human soldiers, but does the invention of riot control drones make it more likely that citizens could lose their vital right to protest?

Other riot control drones are equipped to fire rubber bullets, which are intended to cause pain but not to kill. However, they do sometimes cause serious injuries. One drone currently in development is equipped with tasers. Tasers fire small arrow-like electric devices, which fix in a person's skin and give them an electric shock. Tasers cause pain and make the person's muscles shake uncontrollably. Tasers do not usually do lasting harm, but they have occasionally caused deaths by accidentally triggering heart attacks.

Dogo

The Dogo robot can fire a Glock pistol loaded with real bullets. It can also be armed with nonlethal weapons, such as an intense light to dazzle targets. Glock pistols make up 65 percent of the handguns used by U.S. police officers, and are also used by the police forces of many other countries. Dogo is the first robot to be armed with one. The decision to fire the gun can only be made by the robot's human operator. The human can fix Dogo's laser sight on a person by touching their image as it appears on the control screen. A laser sight uses a narrow beam of light to pinpoint targets with great accuracy. The light is a safety feature that allows the human operator to know that the right person has been pinpointed.

Dogo is equipped and programmed in a similar way to surveillance robots. It has eight video cameras, including cameras on its sides and rear, to give its human operator a full picture of the robot's surroundings. These cameras can switch to infrared when light conditions are low, providing thermal images. Dogo's computer can process all these different images at once, building up a complete map of its surroundings.

Dogo is made from materials that are lightweight but immensely strong and hardwearing. These materials include metals and rubbers that have been given added strength by being combined with supermaterials like carbon fibers. These mixed human-made materials are called composites. Dogo is small and light enough to be carried under the arm of a police officer before it is set in motion. Then Dogo moves on strong, ridged tracks, so it is less likely to get stuck on uneven ground.

Dogo demonstrates how its dazzling light could disable a suspect.

ROBOT REVOLUTION

In the future, it is possible that all combat, both by police forces and armies, will be carried out by completely autonomous robots. Although the U.S. military currently forbids the use of fully autonomous robots to fire weapons, the government is planning for the future. The government has tasked pioneering robotics experts with the job of coming up with an algorithm (a set of mathematical rules) that would allow robots to judge the difference between right and wrong. This reasoning would be a form of artificial intelligence, giving any robot the ability to make moral decisions. In principle, it would give robots the ability to choose whether or not to take a human life.

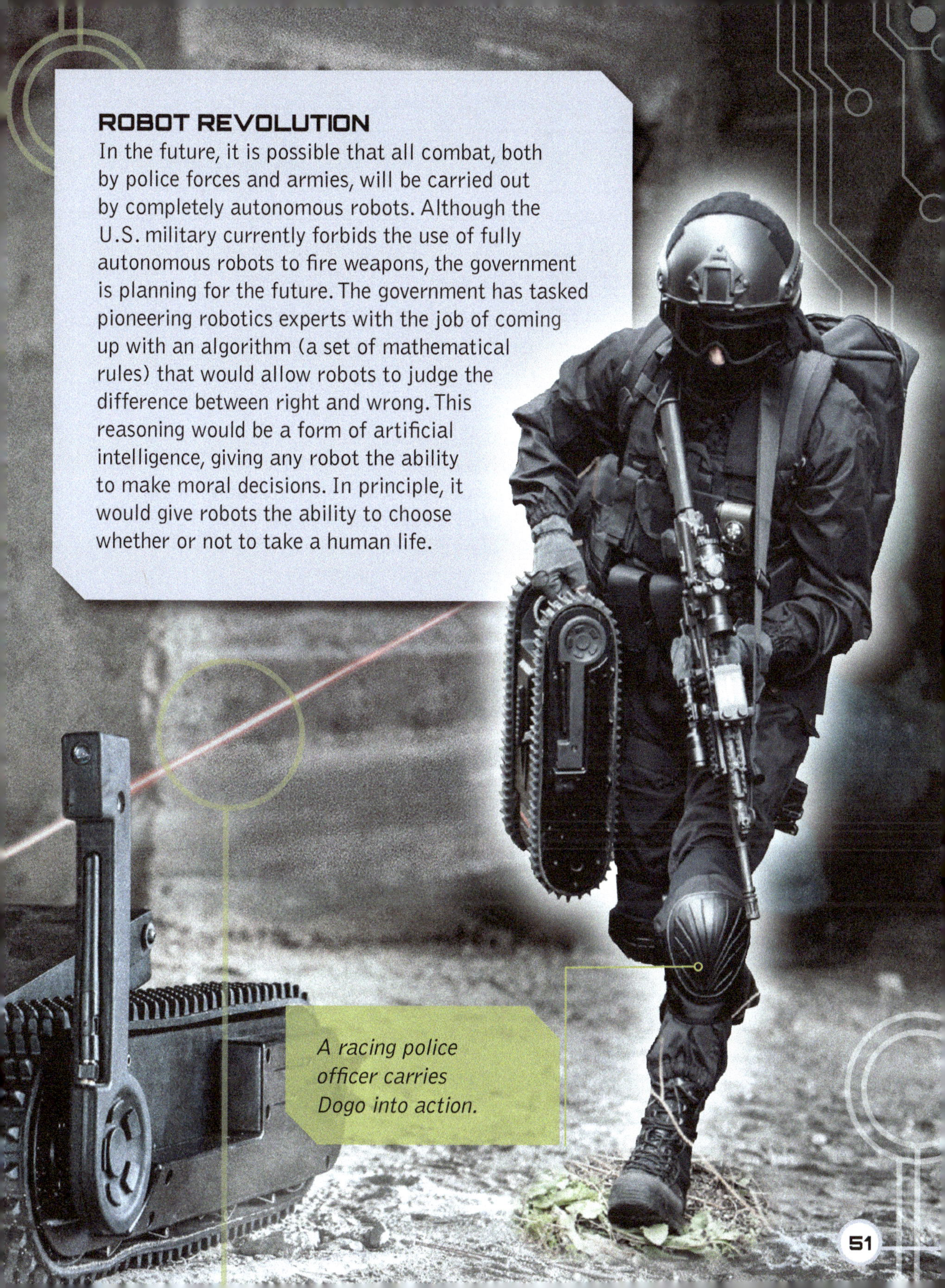

A racing police officer carries Dogo into action.

CHAPTER 6

ON PATROL

An important job of any police force is to patrol the streets, keeping watch for lawbreakers and making people feel safe. This is an area where robots are starting to get to work. Pioneering patrol robots are appearing around the world.

It is important that patrol robots are able to interact with people. Those people might be lost children, tourists asking for directions, or law-breakers. In order to interact, patrol robots need sensors that allow them to see and hear humans. They also need speakers so they can give directions or instructions. In particular, interactive robots need sensors and programs that allow them to understand human speech.

Understanding Speech

To understand speech, a robot needs a microphone and a speech recognition program. Human speech has patterns of loud and soft sounds. Vowels are softer sounds than consonants. A consonant like a "t" is a sudden loud sound. Speech recognition software compares the patterns of loud and soft sounds picked up by its microphone with the sounds in its database. Its database contains around 50 phonemes, the speech sounds that make up the English language, like "ai," "oi," "k," "s," and "ea." Phonemes have no meaning on their own, but once they have been identified, the speech recognition program matches different combinations of phonemes with the words in its database.

Simple talking robots may respond with preprogrammed words and phrases. A basic patrol robot might reply to any inquiry with a polite, "How can I help you?" More complex talking robots have artificial intelligence programs that not only allow them to put together relevant answers to questions but to get better at responding to them. They do this by memorizing the success or failure of past answers.

This robot has built-in speech recognition software.

ROBOT REVOLUTION

Five huge aluminum robots are being used to direct the traffic in the city of Kinshasa, in the Democratic Republic of Congo, Africa. This is a city where unruly drivers often ignore traffic rules, despite patrols by human traffic police. The robots are equipped with changing lights to act as traffic lights. They also wave their arms to signal direction. Their rotating chests have cameras that beam videos of the traffic to police stations. The robots' size and mildly frightening appearance have been successful in making motorists obey the law. Since the robots have been introduced, there have been fewer accidents on the intersections they police.

Engineers put a lot of thought into the faces of robots that interact with people.

Robocops

The city of Dubai was the first city in the world to introduce a full team of robotic police officers. The fully autonomous robots started patrols in 2017. These robocops are humanoid robots, although they do not have legs. The reason for this is that even the most advanced walking robots are currently quite easy to push over, which would not be ideal for a police robot. The Dubai robot balances on a secure pedestal, and moves around on wheels.

The Dubai robocop is not intended to carry out arrests. It has a touchscreen on its chest, which can be used by the public to report crimes they have witnessed, or to pay fines for traffic offenses and parking tickets. The robot also has a microphone that is linked to the central Dubai police call center. Using it, people can report crimes by talking directly with a human who is trained to give the right help. The robot can also scan faces, running them through a database of wanted criminals. If it found a match, it would alert human police officers, who would be able to locate the person by the robot's current location provided by its GPS.

Officers who patrol the streets are highly trained to respond to any situation. Many people wonder if a robot could effectively and safely take over such a job.

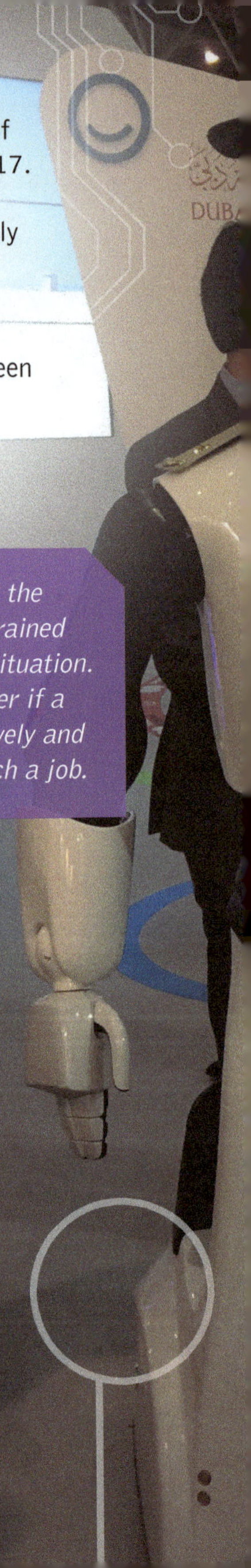

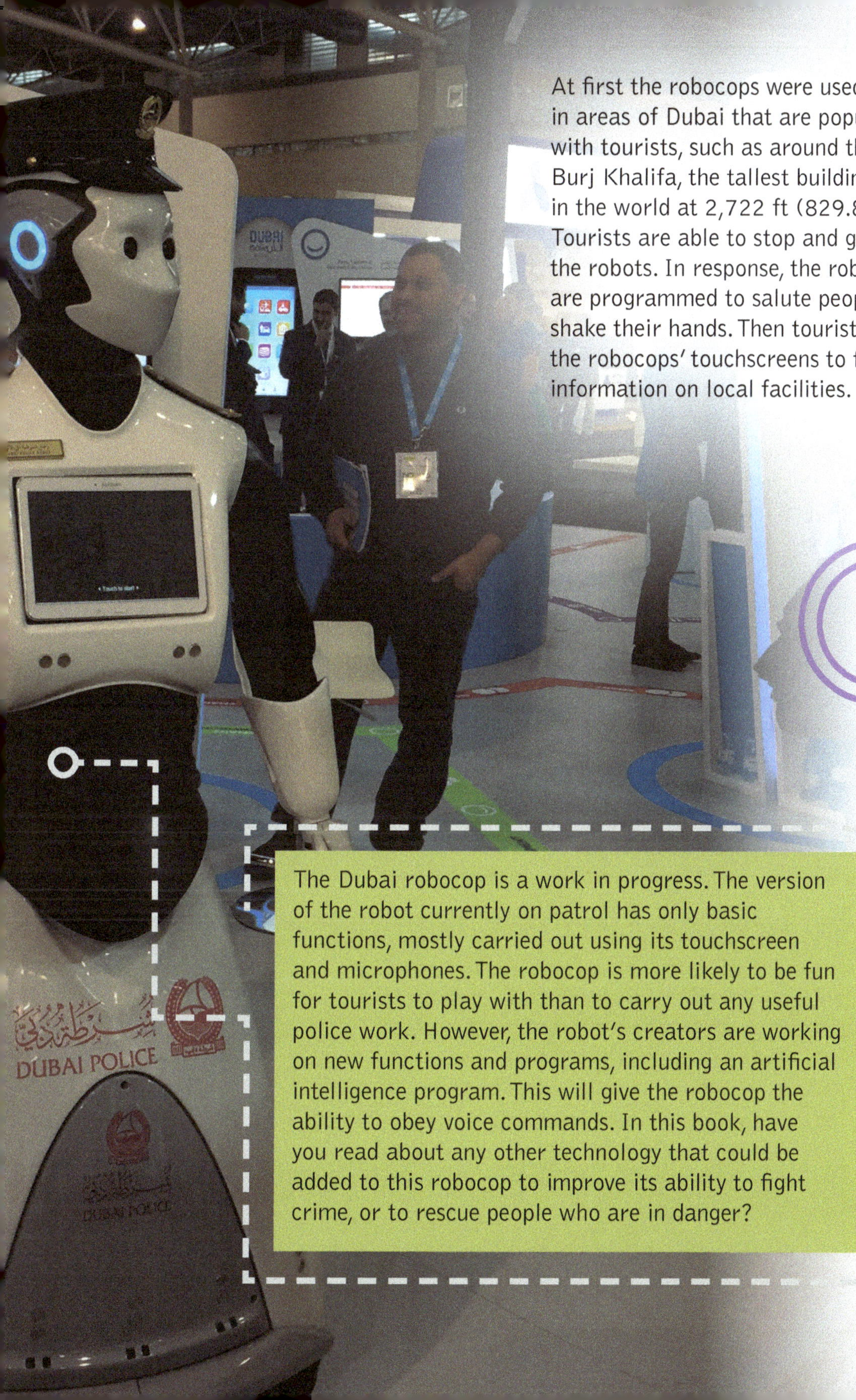

At first the robocops were used only in areas of Dubai that are popular with tourists, such as around the Burj Khalifa, the tallest building in the world at 2,722 ft (829.8 m). Tourists are able to stop and greet the robots. In response, the robocops are programmed to salute people and shake their hands. Then tourists can use the robocops' touchscreens to find out information on local facilities.

The Dubai robocop is a work in progress. The version of the robot currently on patrol has only basic functions, mostly carried out using its touchscreen and microphones. The robocop is more likely to be fun for tourists to play with than to carry out any useful police work. However, the robot's creators are working on new functions and programs, including an artificial intelligence program. This will give the robocop the ability to obey voice commands. In this book, have you read about any other technology that could be added to this robocop to improve its ability to fight crime, or to rescue people who are in danger?

Telepresence is a technology that allows a human to guide a robot by remote control, to see through its cameras, and hear through its microphones. In addition, the human operator's face can often (but not always) be seen on a screen on the robot's "face" or "body," while the human's voice can be heard through the robot's speakers. This makes a telepresence robot not only the eyes, ears, and hands of its human operator, but their face and voice as well.

Telepresence Police Officer

A team of robotics experts at Discovery Lab, part of Florida International University, is working on a telepresence police robot. The telebot will be humanoid, but will move on two sturdy wheels rather than legs. It will have a video camera in its chest, a microphone, and will also have sensors that allow it to sense touch, by picking up on pressure on its surface.

The idea is that the telebot will be operated by police officers and army veterans who have been injured on duty and are now in a wheelchair or not as able bodied as they once were. Thousands of police officers are forced to retire every year because of disability. Around 180,000 veterans of the wars in Iraq and Afghanistan are registered as disabled. After their injuries, these men and women have trouble finding jobs as fulfilling as the jobs they once had. By operating a telepresence robot, these veterans can use their skills to great effect. Rather than the public being faced with a fully autonomous robot that has few functions, as with Dubai's robocops, these telebots would have the brains of highly trained humans. Whereas many robots, particularly industrial robots, are criticized for taking jobs from human workers, these robots would actually enable human workers to get back to work.

Telepresence police robots could provide work for wounded veterans.

Although using telepresence robots for policing is a brand-new idea, telepresence technology is already used to let some people do their jobs from a distance. Telepresence robots are sometimes used when employees want to hold a meeting with colleagues on the other side of the world. A few hundred telepresence robots are already employed in education, so teachers can give lessons in remote schools or to children who are confined to bed. Can you think of any other uses for telepresence robots?

If a business wants to protect its offices, factories, or grounds, it employs a team of human security guards. The team takes turns working through the night, weekends, and holidays. An alternative is to employ a team of robotic security guards, who will never get bored or fall asleep.

K5 Robot Guards

One option is a team of K5 fully autonomous robotic guards. These robots, and others like them, could also be employed by police forces. The K5 has video cameras positioned all around its body, so it gets a 360 degree view of its environment. Thermal imaging cameras let it see in the dark and reveal the warmth of human bodies. Sixteen microphones pick up conversations or suspicious sounds like breaking glass.

All the data collected by the robot's sensors is processed through its computer, which highlights details that are out of place or unusual. The K5 also memorizes all the car license plates it sees, and scans human faces, looking for known criminals. In the future, new versions of the K5 will have a metal detector to spot guns hidden in someone's clothes or bags. When a K5 notices something suspicious, it sends an alert to a control center monitored by humans. Humans can then make the decisions that affect the safety of other humans.

To avoid collisions, a K5 has stereovision cameras to judge distances, and LIDAR to figure out how fast objects and people are approaching. Although a K5 can move at 18 mph (28.8 kph), it usually keeps to a speed of 1–3 mph (1.6–4.8 kph) to avoid injury to humans. When its battery is running down, a K5 automatically goes to a recharging station.

A K5 is covered in a tough, shiny outer shell that is hard to vandalize.

Slightly smaller than its sister robot, the K3 is designed for use indoors, in malls and offices. It has more than 30 sensors, including five cameras.

ROBOT REVOLUTION

Robot guards are patrolling the corridors in Pohang prison in South Korea. This is the first time that robots have been employed for such a job. Using their cameras and microphones, the robotic guards monitor prisoners' behavior. A pioneering feature of the robots is that their programs can spot the signs of someone misbehaving or someone who is feeling extreme sadness or anger. At a basic level, this is accomplished by the robots being taught to recognize "normal" behavior by the level of sound and amount of movement. The robots can then spot behavior that is different. When unusual behavior is spotted, human guards are alerted.

Armored Exosuits

An exosuit is a wearable robot that gives the user extra muscle strength. "Exo" is short for exoskeleton, which is the name for the tough outer shell of soft-bodied animals like crabs. Today, exosuits are used largely in medicine. Although they are a very new invention, pioneering exosuits are already making a difference by helping people with muscle damage to walk again. One day soon, perhaps, exosuits will be worn by police officers to make them stronger and run faster.

Sensors in an exosuit detect the user's movement. Usually, sensors are placed on the user's skin. They pick up the nerve signals that the brain sends to the muscles, telling them to move. The signals can be felt faintly on the skin's surface, and the exosuit is programmed to recognize exactly what motion the user is about to make. The exosuit's actuators, perhaps electric motors, then start to work. Actuators are a robot's muscles. The actuators boost the user's movements by giving them extra muscle power. As a result, a small leg movement becomes a powerful leg movement. As exosuits get better and smarter, they could help users to run really fast without getting tired. This would be a great advantage for police officers when chasing suspects.

In addition, exosuits could give their wearers a tough outer layer, like armor. Police officers already often wear bulletproof vests made of extremely strong materials like Kevlar. Kevlar is a human-made fiber that is five times stronger than steel. If exosuits covered the entire body and head with a material like Kevlar, police officers could be truly superhuman. Combined with pioneering autonomous robots, the future of law enforcement may look very different.

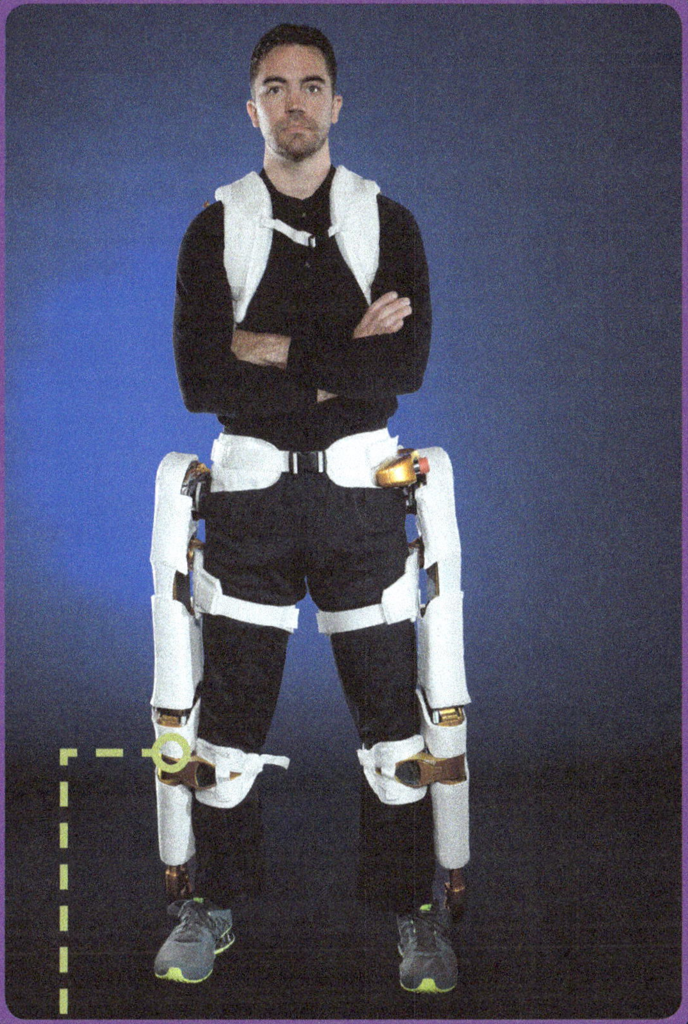

A leg exosuit allows the wearer to walk farther and faster.

The National Aeronautics and Space Administration (NASA) is developing the XI robotic exoskeleton for use by its astronauts, as well as people on Earth who are paralyzed. The exosuit is worn over the legs, attached by a harness around the shoulders. There are ten motorized joints: one in each hip, one in each knee, and three in each foot. The U.S. military is also designing its own exosuits, which would include body armor and GPS. Using the information in this book, design your own exosuit. What extra features might be useful for police officers? Could exosuits change the nature of policing forever?

GLOSSARY

absorbent Able to soak up.

actuators Devices that change electrical energy into movement.

artificial intelligence The ability of a machine to perform tasks that normally require human intelligence, such as understanding speech.

automatically By itself; with no human control.

autonomous Able to act independently.

civil liberties A person's rights within society.

computer A machine that carries out a set of instructions called a program.

data Information.

defuse Prevent from exploding.

detonator The part of a bomb that triggers the explosion.

digital Information or signals expressed as a pattern of 0s and 1s.

drones Driverless aircraft that can navigate independently.

electric motor Machine that changes electrical energy into movement.

electronic circuits Loops around which electrical current can travel.

end effector The device at the end of a robotic arm.

Global Positioning System (GPS) A system that uses signals from satellites to determine a location.

hostages People held prisoner until demands are met.

humanoid Similar in shape to a human.

hydraulics A system operated by moving and compressing liquid.

infrared Energy that humans cannot see.

mobile Able to move from place to place.

nonlethal Something that might harm but does not kill.

pneumatic A system operated by moving and compressing gas.

program A set of ordered instructions.

projectiles Objects fired from a gun.

radar A system that uses radio waves to detect large objects like ships and aircraft.

radioactive Giving off energy in the form of radiation.

radio waves A form of energy that is used for sending invisible signals through the air.

sensors Devices that detect something and then react to it.

sonar A system that uses sound waves to detect something underwater.

stereovision Able to perceive three dimensions.

surveillance Keeping watch on something.

telepresence Technologies that allow a person to feel as if they are present, or to give the appearance of being present.

terrorists People who use violence to achieve their goals.

thermal image An image produced by measuring the heat given off by objects and animals.

ultrasonic Using sound waves that cannot be heard by humans.

ultraviolet Energy that humans cannot see.

warrant A legal document that gives police permission to search or arrest someone.

X-ray A form of energy that can pass through some materials.

FOR MORE INFORMATION

Books

Faust, Daniel R. *Military and Police Robots*. New York, NY: PowerKids Press, 2016.

Platt, Charles. *Make: Electronics*. San Francisco, CA: Maker Media, 2015.

Stewart, Melissa. *Robots*. Washington, D.C.: National Geographic Children's Books, 2014.

Ventura, Marne. *The 12 Biggest Breakthroughs in Robotic Technology*. Mankato, MN: 12-Story, 2015.

Websites

Find out what engineers at Harvard University are doing with robots:
http://biodesign.seas.harvard.edu/soft-robotics

Do some more research about robots and what they can do:
www.galileo.org/robotics/intro.html

Take a closer look at drones:
www.kidsdiscover.com/teacherresources/drones-uavs-rescue

Get involved by designing your own robots:
www.wro-usa.org

Publisher's note to educators and parents: Our editors have carefully reviewed these websites to ensure that they are suitable for students. Many websites change frequently, however, and we cannot guarantee that a site's future contents will continue to meet our high standards of quality and educational value. Be advised that students should be closely supervised whenever they access the Internet.

INDEX